RHINOCEROSES

BY JUDITH JANGO-COHEN

BENCHMARK BOOKS

MARSHALL CAVENDISH
NEW YORK

Series Consultant
James Doherty
General Curator
Bronx Zoo, New York

For Julie Dunlap, nature lover and friend
–j.j.c.

Benchmark Books
Marshall Cavendish
99 White Plains Road
Tarrytown, NY 10591-9001
www.marshallcavendish.us

Library of Congress Cataloging-in-Publication Data

Jango-Cohen, Judith.
Rhinoceroses / Judith Jango-Cohen.
p. cm. – (Animals, animals)
Includes bibliographical references and index.
ISBN 0-7614-1753-2
1. Rhinoceroses–Juvenile literature. I. Title. II. Series.

QL737.U63J36 2004
599.66'8–dc22
2004000839

Photo Research Joan Meisel

Cover photo: Roland Seitre/Peter Arnold, Inc.

Photographs in this book are used by permission and through the courtesy of: *Corbis*: Terry Whittaker/Frank Lane Picture Agency, 14; Peter Johnson, 28. *Peter Arnold, Inc.*: Roland Seitre/BIOS, 4, 8 (top), 9 (bottom), 12–13, 22, 26;Norbert Wu, 6; Martin Harvey, 7, 8 (bottom), 10, 11, 16, 20, 30, 33, 34; Alain Compost/BIOS, 9 (top); Fred Bavendam, 9 (center); Albert Visage, 24–25; Gilles Martin/Still Pictures, 36; Jochen Tack/Das Fotoarchiv, 38;Y. Arthus-Bertrand, 42.

Printed in China
3 5 6 4 2

CONTENTS

1
INTRODUCING RHINOCEROSES

In a South African wildlife reserve, a black rhinoceros nips at bushes sprouting from a termite mound. Beneath a tree, a ranger watches the animal with binoculars. From surrounding hills, a warm wind wafts into the valley. It carries the ranger's scent to the rhino. The wary male rhinoceros lifts its head. It sniffs, snorts, and charges. Grabbing a low tree limb, the ranger hoists himself into higher branches. Seconds later, the rhino *bull* is below him. For a while it huffs around the trunk and stomps its hooves. Then, satisfied that it has dispatched the danger, the black rhinoceros trots away.

Africa is home to two of the five types, or *species*, of rhinoceros—the black rhino and the white rhino. While both the black and the white rhino are actually gray in color, they can sometimes appear brown, white, or orange,

THE WORD RHINOCEROS IS FORMED FROM TWO GREEK WORDS—*RHIN* MEANING NOSE AND *KERAS* MEANING HORN.

THE HOOK-LIPPED BLACK RHINO EATS MORE THAN TWO HUNDRED DIFFERENT KINDS OF PLANTS.

depending upon the color of the mud they have rolled in. Both types of African rhinoceros have hairless hides and two horns. One can easily tell them apart by the shape of their mouths.

The black rhinoceros has a pointy upper lip. This lip is *prehensile*, which means it can grab and grasp. Black rhinos use their prehensile lip for *browsing*. They pluck leaves, twigs, and fruit with this muscular upper lip, stuffing the food into their mouths.

6

The African white rhino is a *grazer* with wide, straight-edged lips. Its other name is the square-lipped rhinoceros. A white rhino's mouth moves flat against the ground as it nips off grass. Like all rhinos, the white rhino spends about half its time eating. Plenty of plants are needed to fuel such large, heavy animals.

A WHITE RHINO'S SOFT UPPER LIP FEELS FOR GRASS BLADES, WHILE ITS TOUGH LOWER LIP NIPS THEM OFF.

RHINOCEROS SPECIES

HERE ARE THE FIVE RHINOCEROS SPECIES WITH APPROXIMATE
ADULT WEIGHT AND HEIGHT AT THE SHOULDER.

White Rhinoceros
6,000 pounds (2,722 kg)
6 feet (1.8m)

Black Rhinoceros
3,000 pounds (1,361 kg)
5.5 feet (1.7m)

Javan Rhinoceros
3,000 pounds (1,361 kg)
5.5 feet (1.7m)

Indian Rhinoceros
6,000 pounds (2,722 kg)
6.5 feet (2m)

Sumatran Rhinoceros
2,000 pounds (907 kg)
5 feet (1.5m)

RHINOS CAN SLEEP LYING DOWN OR STANDING UP.

Three other rhinoceros species live in Asia. They are the Javan, Sumatran, and Indian. Indian rhinos are also called Asian greater one–horned rhinos. This is a more accurate name since this species lives both in India and in the neighboring nation of Nepal. Its preferred *habitat* is flooded plains and swampy grasslands. It often feeds neck–deep in

RHINOCEROSES RARELY STRAY FAR FROM WATER. THEY MAY TRAVEL UP TO 16 MILES (25 KM) IN A DAY TO FIND WATER AND FOOD.

water, slimy plants dripping from its mouth. Unlike other rhinos, its hide is dotted with knobby bumps.

The smaller Javan rhinoceros is also known as the Asian lesser one-horned rhino. Only about seventy of these rhinos survive in rain forests today. Approximately sixty inhabit the Indonesian island of Java, and about half a dozen live in Vietnam. Both Javan and Indian rhinos have just one horn. Female Javan rhinos may have just a little nub, or no horn at all.

RHINOCEROSES HAVE A REPUTATION FOR BEING DANGEROUS, BUT IN GENERAL THEY ARE PEACEFUL AND EVEN TIMID UNLESS THEY ARE THREATENED.

THE SUMATRAN IS THE ONLY ASIAN RHINO WITH TWO HORNS. THE FRONT HORN IS USUALLY THE LONGEST.

The only Asian species with two horns is the Sumatran rhinoceros. About three hundred live in rain forests on the Indonesian island of Sumatra, the Malay Peninsula, and the island of Borneo. This species is quite different from its relatives, with reddish–brown hair covering its hide. It is also the runt of the rhinos, weighing about 2,000 pounds (910 kg). Indian and white rhinos may weigh three times as much.

All rhinoceroses are big-boned and bulky. But these hulking animals are bulging with muscle–not fat. They are equipped with stiff, spiky horns, which they sharpen on trees and rocks. People who work with rhinoceroses, such as scientists and rangers, quickly learn to respect them. This is also true of animals that live alongside rhinoceroses.

2
HORNS, HIDE, AND HOOVES

A lion crouches at the edge of a pond, lapping up water. Lipp! Plippp! Two white rhinos approach. The lion looks up. Without another sip, it turns to leave. Pausing, the lion glances over its shoulder. Both rhinos stop, stare, and stomp their feet. Reluctantly, the lion pads away.

Even the lofty lion will not challenge a mature, healthy rhinoceros. The rhino is intimidating with its titanic size and horns that resemble colossal claws. Rhino horns are composed of *keratin*, which also makes up claws, hair, hooves, and nails. Like these other substances, horns will grow back if broken off. White rhinos wield the largest horns of all the species. The record is a front horn that measured over 6 1/2 feet (2m).

Rhinoceroses have many uses for their horns. These pointed prongs are intimidating weapons that discourage animals from tussling with rhinos. If provoked, the rhino may spear its enemies or hook and toss them.

WHEN TWO MALES MEET AT A DISTANCE, THEY TURN THEIR HEADS FROM SIDE TO SIDE, SHOWING OFF THEIR HORNS.

HORNS

SMALL EYES

THICK HIDE

TAIL

SHORT LEGS

Rangers at one South African reserve nicknamed a rhino Poking Polly. When people climbed trees to escape its charges, the rhinoceros would try to yank them out with its horn. Rhinos put their horns to good use by digging for water, plants, and salts. These rugged horns can crack off tree limbs, allowing rhinos to reach tender leaf tips. The rhinoceros also employs this branch–breaking technique to clear trails through tangled brush.

A thick, tough hide ensures that rhinos are not cut by thorny bushes or prickly vines. Rhino skin looks as though it is armored with rigid plates. But this plated

18

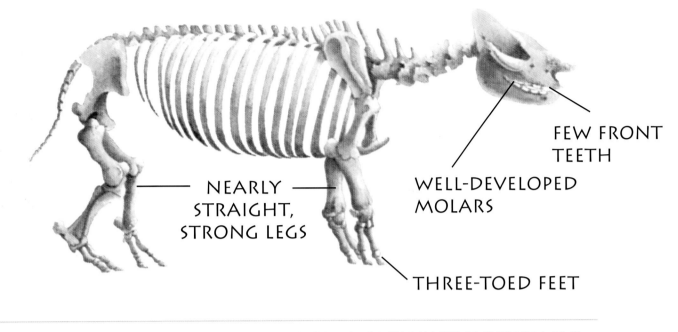

FEW FRONT TEETH

WELL-DEVELOPED MOLARS

NEARLY STRAIGHT, STRONG LEGS

THREE-TOED FEET

LIKE OTHER LARGE, HEAVY ANIMALS, RHINOS HAVE NEARLY STRAIGHT LEGS AND LARGE FEET.

appearance is produced by folds in the hide. Indian and Javan rhinos, with more creases, look more armored than other species. Except for newborn rhinos and the Sumatran rhinoceros, rhino hide is hairless. But all rhinos have fringes of hair on their eyelids and ears, and on the end of their slender tails.

The tail is the only slender part of a rhinoceros. Other herbivores, or plant-eaters, run around on stick-thin legs. But the hefty rhino requires a more sturdy foundation. Its legs are like pillars with three toes that form a clover-shaped base. A hoof shields the tip of each toe. Despite

19

IF TWO ADULT MALE RHINOS MEET FACE-TO-FACE AND ONE DOES NOT BACK DOWN, A FIGHT MAY OCCUR. THE AFRICAN RHINO ATTACKS RIVALS WITH ITS HORNS, FIRST USING ITS FRONT HORN LIKE A CLUB THEN JABBING WITH THE TIP.

their plodding appearance, rhinos can run about twice as fast as the average human. If threatened, they can sprint off at 30 miles per hour (50 km/hr).

Rhinos are always on the alert for danger. Even while asleep, their perky ears pivot around picking up any suspicious sound. Their tiny eyes are not too reliable, so if rhinos hear something unusual they locate it with their noses. Rhinos have a remarkable sense of smell. Large nasal passages in their skulls detect odors. These chambers take up more skull space than the brain.

Rhinos use their keen sense of smell not only for protection, but also to communicate with each other. Black, white, and Javan bull rhinos outline their territories with urine. Black and white rhinos also fortify their borders with stacks of dung. Passing rhinos interpret these scent signs to mean "Private Property–Keep Out!" All rhino species have community dung heaps, where neighboring rhinos deposit their droppings. These smelly piles are found in common areas like watering holes and wallows. Experiments have proven that rhinos can distinguish one another by the scent of the dung. With a sniff of these mounds, a rhinoceros can figure out who has been by.

3
MUD BATHS AND BACK SCRATCHES

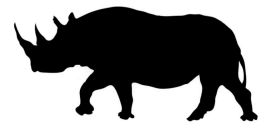

It is a busy day at the water hole. Elephants slosh on the muddy shallows, splashing waves of water. They waggle their ears and trumpet as they soak in the soft mud. A little black rhino prances up to the pool, bucking and tossing its head. It scampers backward, then dashes forward again. As ripples of water roll toward its toes, the baby scrambles away. Although rhino calves may be intimidated by the commotion, adult rhinos find the water hole relaxing. They drink their fill and wallow until they are covered with muck. Wallowing keeps them cool and protects their hide from sunburn. Moist mud softens a rhino's skin and prevents it from cracking. The thick coating also smothers blood-sucking ticks and blocks insects from stinging.

AS MOIST MUD DRIES, IT DRAWS HEAT AWAY FROM A RHINO'S BODY.

23

LONG AGO, PEOPLE LIVING IN JUNGLES FOLLOWED RHINOC-EROS TRAILS TO FIND WATER.

RHINOS, ELEPHANTS, AND HIPPOS ARE ALL PACHYDERMS, WHICH MEANS
THICK-SKINNED.

Birds also help a rhinoceros in its battle against biting insects. In Africa, oxpeckers skitter over a rhino's wide sides plucking out ticks and picking off worms, fleas, and flies. In Asia, Indian rhinos get a hand from mynah birds. Turtles do their part too. While a rhinoceros is in the water, turtles climb aboard its back or dive underwater nipping ticks off its skin.

A rhinoceros also keeps its hide healthy by rubbing against rocks and trees. Favorite rubbing posts are worn smooth. Scratching knocks scabs, skin flakes, and bugs off a rhino's hide. Unfortunately, there is one spot behind a rhino's front legs that is tricky to reach. Black rhinos often have infected sores there.

Rubbing posts, water holes, and wallows are crucial to a rhino's survival. Rhinos from neighboring *territories* peacefully share these places. Aside from meeting in these common areas, rhinoceros bulls stick to their own territories.

A RHINOCEROS FAITHFULLY FOLLOWS THE SAME TRAILS TO ITS WATER HOLES, MUD WALLOWS, AND FEEDING GROUNDS. OTHER ANIMALS USE THESE CONVENIENT CLEARINGS. PEOPLE DO TOO. ON JAVA, SOME ANCIENT RHINO TRAILS ARE NOW MODERN ROADS.

A RED-BILLED OXPECKER SITS ON THE NOSE OF A WHITE RHINOCEROS.

Some bulls allow immature males and old bulls to live in their territories. As long as these rhinos accept their lower position, the bull lets them stay. But if a young male tries to take over, there will be a showdown.

4
RHINO REPRODUCTION

Two white rhinos, an adult bull and a young male, stand nose to nose. Lowering their heads, they brush their horns against the ground. The rhinos glare, each holding its ground. Although there is not much action, there is a lot of noise. The larger bull lets out a low, rumbling growl. The young male whines. Sensing that it is not up to the challenge the younger rhino backs away. One day it may guard its own territory. But for now the bigger bull has defended its sleeping area, feeding grounds, and also its breeding rights. When a female, or *cow* passes through, only the older male will have the right to mate.

Bulls attempt to keep a cow in their territory if she is ready to mate. But after mating, the cow goes off on its own. Fifteen or sixteen months later, it gives birth–usually to a single calf. Mother rhinos hide their young in tall

WHITE RHINO CALVES WEIGH 100 POUNDS (45KG) OR MORE AT BIRTH.

grass or dense brush. Like all *mammals*, the mother feeds its baby milk. Bit by bit the calf experiments with eating plants. But it continues to nurse for a year or two.

When the mother feels ready, it takes its calf from the protected area. If the two become separated, their sense of smell will guide them back together. Calves join their mothers at water holes and wallows. But a mud bath is not safe for the calf until it is strong enough to climb out.

Rhino calves are easy *prey* for predators. Asian rhinos defend their young from tigers, while African rhinos fend off lions and spotted hyenas. Spotted hyenas are the most successful at hunting rhino calves. They work in groups and attack from all sides.

A mother rhinoceros is a ferocious obstacle for any predator, so most calves survive. They live alongside their mothers for two to five years, until a new calf is born.

AN ELEPHANT'S HELP

A BLACK RHINO CALF BECAME TRAPPED IN A DEEP MUD HOLE IN KENYA. ITS MOTHER COULD NOT HELP. BUT AN ADULT ELEPHANT CAME TO THE BABY'S AID. THE ELEPHANT KNELT DOWN AND TRIED TO LIFT THE CALF OUT WITH ITS STURDY TUSKS.

THIS RHINO CALF'S MINIATURE HORN WILL CONTINUE TO GROW ALL ITS LIFE.

BLACK RHINOS TAKE ABOUT SEVEN YEARS TO REACH FULL GROWTH.

Then the mother chases the young rhino away, perhaps to prevent it from harming the baby. At first young rhinos do not feel comfortable living on their own. Black rhinos often pair up with another young rhino. White rhinos may do the same or they may join a female without a calf. Groups of these white rhino "aunts" and calves sometimes link together.

Eventually, young rhinos go off on their own. They feed, drink, wallow, scratch, and watch for danger. They have lived much this same way for about 50 million years.

5
RHINO SURVIVAL

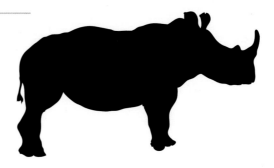

Deep in the Lascaux Cave in France stands a mighty rhinoceros. It is a painting that has stared from cave walls for 17,000 years. The portrait shows a wooly rhinoceros with two pointy horns and a raised tail. The rhino has just punctured the belly of a bison, which lies dead.

Prehistoric people both feared and respected the rhinoceros. They may also have believed it had magical powers. In another cave in France, there is a painting of a creature with a rhinoceros head and a human body.

People do not believe in magical rhinos today. But some believe that powerful medicines can be made from rhinoceros horn. The five hundred–year–old *Encyclopedia of Chinese Medicine*, still in use today, recommends rhino horn for a variety of illnesses. The horn may be ground to a powder and mixed with butter or honey. It may also be

INDIAN RHINOS ARE THE MOST POPULAR ATTRACTION IN NEPAL'S ROYAL CHITWAN NATIONAL PARK.

THE SPEED AT WHICH A BROKEN HORN GROWS BACK DEPENDS UPON THE AGE, SEX, AND SPECIES OF THE RHINOCEROS.

boiled in water to make a medicinal tea. Throughout Asia, rhinoceros horn is prescribed to reduce fever, to stop nosebleeds, and to cure colds and headaches.

In Yemen, south of Saudi Arabia, people also seek rhino horn. Here it is used for ornate dagger handles. Men in Yemen wear curved daggers tucked into fancy sheaths during religious ceremonies. During the 1900s, the demand for rhino horn remedies and decorated dagger handles rose. Hunters were killing all species of rhinoceros, and cutting off their horns. By the end of the century, rhinoceros horn was worth more money than gold. As the clamoring for rhinoceros horn increased, rhino populations plummeted.

Rhinoceros numbers also declined during this period because a growing human population was taking over their habitat. In Sumatra, tropical forest was cut down to develop rubber plantations. Tea plantations took over the living space of the Indian rhino. Farmlands spread throughout Africa. Governments paid people to kill the remaining rhinos. They wanted to prevent the big beasts from stomping through the fields and chomping on the crops. In 1948, a single hunter killed five hundred rhinos in Africa.

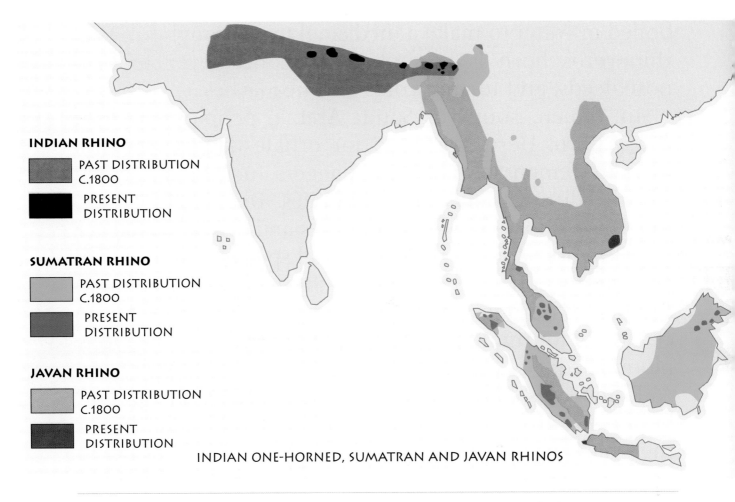

INDIAN RHINO

PAST DISTRIBUTION
C.1800

PRESENT
DISTRIBUTION

SUMATRAN RHINO

PAST DISTRIBUTION
C.1800

PRESENT
DISTRIBUTION

JAVAN RHINO

PAST DISTRIBUTION
C.1800

PRESENT
DISTRIBUTION

INDIAN ONE-HORNED, SUMATRAN AND JAVAN RHINOS

INDIAN ONE-HORNED, SUMATRAN, AND JAVAN RHINOCEROSES

This unchecked slaughter is now a thing of the past. Laws regulate hunting these *endangered* animals. Since 1977, international regulations have prohibited selling and trading rhinoceros horns or other body parts.

40

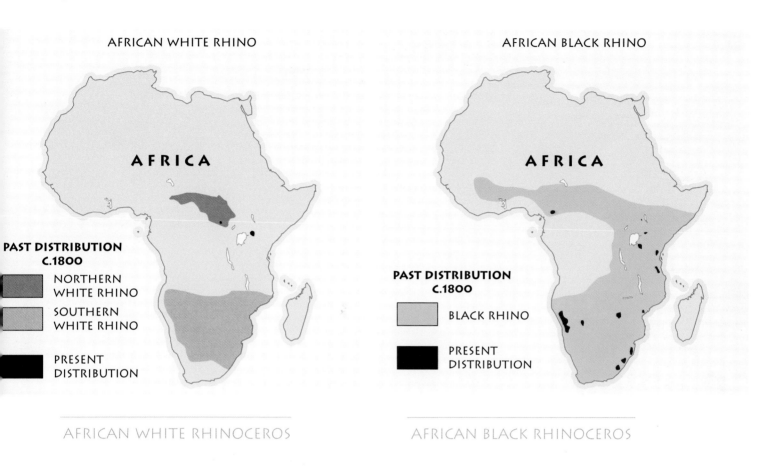

AFRICAN WHITE RHINO

AFRICA

PAST DISTRIBUTION C.1800

NORTHERN WHITE RHINO

SOUTHERN WHITE RHINO

PRESENT DISTRIBUTION

AFRICAN WHITE RHINOCEROS

AFRICAN BLACK RHINO

AFRICA

PAST DISTRIBUTION C.1800

BLACK RHINO

PRESENT DISTRIBUTION

AFRICAN BLACK RHINOCEROS

Most rhinos live in areas where they are guarded against illegal hunters, called *poachers*. These areas may be owned by governments or by private organizations. When these protected places become overcrowded, some rhinos are moved elsewhere. Rhinos have now been reintroduced to regions from which they had disappeared.

A POWERFUL SENSE OF SMELL HELPS RHINOS DETECT PREDATORS—EVEN AFTER DARK.

Conservationists, people who work to preserve natural resources, are working to save the rhinoceros by educating people. They are showing communities that living rhinos are worth more than dead ones. Tourists, who come to see the rhinos, bring money. Tourist dollars can be used to build schools and to dig wells for villages.

Some people continue to poach because they are poor and hungry. An African conservation society in Zambia is working on this problem. The society runs a program to teach skills like beekeeping and pottery–making to former poachers. Villagers also learn farming methods that yield more crops. One man, a poacher since the age of thirteen, once had no skills to earn a living. Now he has an education and more food than ever to feed his seven children. He says he will never poach again. Conservationists are hoping that people will find ways to save room for the rhino. It is a fellow creature that shares our increasingly crowded planet. And it may pay to remember that the rhinoceros was here first.

browse: To eat plant materials such as leaves, fruits, flowers, and seeds.

bull: An adult male rhinoceros.

conservationists: People who work to protect living things and their habitats.

cow: An adult female rhinoceros.

endangered: Threatened with dying out.

graze: To eat grass and other low-growing plants.

habitat: The natural surroundings or environment where an animal lives.

herbivore: An animal that feeds chiefly on plants.

keratin: A tough protein that makes up claws, horns, hooves, nails, and hair.

mammal: A warm-blooded animal with a backbone, that has fur or hair, gives birth to live young, and makes milk to feed its young.

poacher: A person who illegally hunts and kills animals.

prehensile: Able to grasp or wrap around something.

prey: An animal that is hunted and eaten by other animals.

species: A particular type of living thing.

territory: An area that an animal defends as its own for feeding and mating.

BOOKS

Arnold, Caroline. *Rhino*. New York: Morrow Junior Books, 1995.

Cole, Melissa. *Rhinos*. Farmington Hills, Michigan: Blackbirch Press, 2002.

Harman, Amanda. *Rhinoceroses*. Tarrytown, New York: Benchmark Books, 1997.

Holmes, Kevin J. *Rhinos*. Mankato, Minnesota: Bridgestone Books, 2000.

Penny, Malcolm. *Black Rhino*. Austin, Texas: Raintree Steck-Vaughn, 2001.

Stewart, Melissa. *Rhinoceroses*. New York: Children's Press, 2002.

Walker, Sally M. *Rhinos*. Minneapolis, Minnesota: Carolrhoda Books, 1996.

WEB SITES

Animalbytes: Rhinoceros
www.sandiegozoo.org/animalbytes/t-rhinoceros.html

In the Wild: Africa (Black Rhinoceros)
www.bagheera.com/inthewild/van_anim_rhino.htm

International Rhino Foundation
www.rhinos-irf.org

SOS Rhino
www.sosrhino.org

South Africa: Rhinoceros
www.sa-venues.com/wildlife/wildlife_rhino.htm

World Wildlife Fund: Endangered Species
www.worldwildlife.org/species/species.cfm

FIND OUT MORE

VIDEOS

Growing Up Wild: Tons of Fun Time Life Video, 1992.

Nature's Newborn: White Rhino, Jackal, Monkey. Diamond Entertainment Corp., 1994.

The Rhino War. National Geographic, 1987.

ABOUT THE AUTHOR

Judith Jango-Cohen's intimate knowledge of nature comes from years of outdoor exploration. She has observed and photographed animals, plants, and geological formations in swamps, canyons, caves, and glaciers. Her twenty-eight children's books reflect these experiences. They have been listed in Best Books for Children, recommended by the National Science Teachers Association, and chosen for the Children's Literature Choice List. You can find photos from the many trips she has taken with her family at www.agpix.com/cohen.

Page numbers for illustrations are in **boldface.**